THEN AND THERE SERIES
GENERAL EDITOR
MARJORIE REEVES

Weavers and Outworkers in Victorian Times

PETER SEARBY

Illustrated from contemporary sources

LONGMAN

LONGMAN GROUP LIMITED
London
*Associated companies, branches and representatives
throughout the world*

First published 1980
ISBN 0 582 23017 9

Set in 11/12½ Baskerville. Monophoto 169

*Printed in Hong Kong by
Wilture Enterprises (International) Ltd.*

Contents

To the Reader

This book centres on the life of one man, Joseph Gutteridge, who was a weaver in Coventry one hundred years ago. His hours of work were long and heavy. In his leisure he made violins out of old pieces of wood, experimented with electricity and collected plants and fossils; he had a little 'museum' in the parlour of his house.

You would not find many weavers in Queen Victoria's reign with hobbies like these, but many men in Coventry and other Victorian towns had jobs like Gutteridge's.

When we read about industry at this time, we usually learn about factories – for example, cotton factories – and the fact that goods could be made more cheaply in them. In the end factories were built for every industry, but for a long time in the nineteenth century many common things were not made in factories, but in workshops that were part of houses; examples are nails, needles, boots and shoes, and also silk ribbons, which were woven in Coventry by Joseph Gutteridge and others.

Coventry weavers, like many *outdoor* workers, hated working in factories and tried to stop them being built. Their fight against factories is part of this book. They also fought against 'free trade' which we hear about so much in the middle of the nineteenth century. This was supposed to help people, but in Coventry free trade ruined the ribbon industry because in 1860 cheap foreign ribbons were allowed to be *imported*. Coventry people felt that they were being made poorer so that British women could buy cheap ribbons from abroad; this argument reminds us of what is said today about cheap shirts from Hong Kong or shoes from Portugal, which sell for lower prices than British shirts or shoes and so put British workers out of jobs.

But before 1860 many weavers were quite well off, earning 30s (£1.50) a week. This seems little to us, but prices then were much lower than ours. For example, a five-room house could be rented for 4s (20p) a week and a hundredweight (50 kg) of coal cost about 7d (3p). You should multiply these wages and prices by twenty to find their value today. After 1860 wages in Coventry fell by half.

Words printed in *italics* are explained in the Glossary on page 73.

Opposite: *Coventry, a map drawn a few years before Joseph Gutteridge was born*

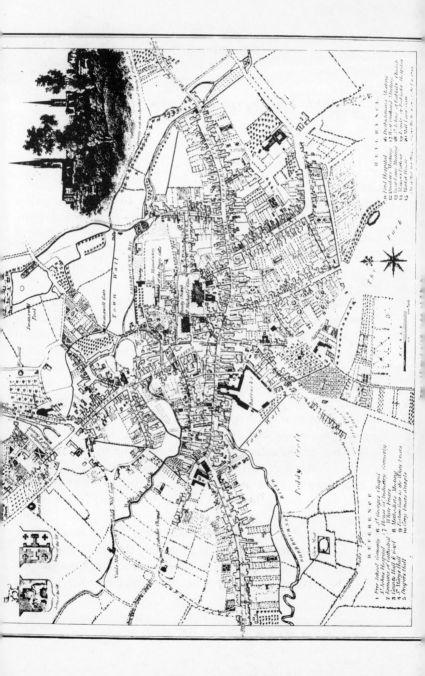

REFERENCE

1 Free School formerly
2 St Johns Hospital
3 Remains of Cathedral
4 Guard Hall & Gaol
5 Draper's Hall
6 St George's Chapel
7 House of Industry formerly
8 White Friars
9 Methodists Meeting
10 Grey Friars Steeple

11 Foul Hospital
12 Quakers Meeting
13 Tower Meeting
14 St James's
15 St Peter's

16 Presbyterian Meeting
17 Independant Meeting
18 St Johns of Jerusalem Parish
19 Remains of Lazar's House
20 Ruins of Kilkulee Hospital

THE PARK

Town Wall
SHERBOURNE RIVER
Swanzey Pool
Broomwell Gate
Hamiltons
Remains of the Priory Castle
Watch Tower Wall
Barracks
Town Wall
Paddy Croft
Corn Mool
SHERBOURNE RIVER

1 Joseph Gutteridge's Life

CHILDHOOD

Joseph Gutteridge was born in 1816 in Coventry. It was a small town by modern standards, with 21,000 inhabitants compared to over 350,000 today. It was only $1\frac{1}{2}$ kilometres across, and fields were within easy reach of all the narrow streets, where black and white Tudor houses overhung piles of filth that were rarely cleared away. Sewers emptied into the Sherbourne, a slow and dirty river that overflowed in winter. People got their drinking water from wells. Life was unhealthy.

When he was five Joseph went to a school kept by an old woman. She taught him to read, and also to sew and knit; with her kindness she calmed down what Joseph called his 'highly excitable and nervous *temperament*'. Later, he went to a much less pleasant school, where boys who made mistakes in their lessons were birched. 'The culprit', wrote Gutteridge many years later, 'was stripped and hoisted on the back of the tallest boy in the school, the master standing by his side with a rod of stout twigs'.

Like many at the time, Joseph learned as much outside school as in it. When he was a child he became interested in natural things around him and collected wild plants. Sometimes he climbed 4 metres up the walls of the city, which were four hundred years old, to gather the ferns and snapdragons growing in the cracks between the sandstone blocks. Often he walked in the fields near the town to collect plants

Opposite: *Coventry, a Victorian drawing of the Town Wall and Cook Street Gate. Notice the ditch on the outside of the wall. Why was the ditch there?*

like wood sage, finding the names for them from the coloured pictures in a book given to him by his father. Joseph sketched and painted pictures of plants or rubbed impressions of leaves with a pencil on very thin paper. Birds were another interest. Joseph used to climb trees to collect their eggs or to capture young birds to train as pets. His magpies were a nuisance to neighbours because they stole small things like thimbles. He tried to teach starlings to repeat words, as parrots do, but all they did was to croak.

Joseph's father and uncles had been soldiers and had played in their regimental bands. In Coventry, they used to meet to play marches together. Joseph listened to his father's music and liked it; he learned to play his father's flute and *piccolo*. While he was still a boy, Joseph also came to like making boxes and bird cages out of wood. He went on doing these things all his life.

Joseph's family was poor and life was hard. His father was a ribbon weaver, working sixty or more hours a week. (Today, children work at school for twenty-five hours a week.) His mother was crippled and Joseph had to cook many meals; after she died his father remarried. Like most children of the time, his schooling ended at thirteen. He had to learn a job. He wanted to become a carpenter, but was forced by his father to become an *apprentice* ribbon weaver. In this way he followed his father and grandfather in the chief trade of the city.

WEAVING

Gutteridge called the *autobiography* he wrote in old age 'Lights and Shadows in the Life of an Artisan', a title that gives a good idea of the ups and downs of his life. Very skilful with his hands, he became one of the best weavers in the city, making the most complicated patterns. But like many other workmen he found his job boring because it did not give his brain enough to do. As an apprentice, pleasure came from walking in the countryside, as early as 4 a.m., before work began at 6 a.m., to collect plants and insects.

4   His father died of *consumption* when Joseph was seventeen.

Afterwards, his many quarrels with his stepmother made him unhappy; she called his plants 'litter' and threw them away. When he was nineteen Gutteridge married, something an apprentice was not supposed to do because he was still learning his job and was looked on as a child. His family and employer were angry. Proud and strong-minded, he took no notice. With only an apprentice's small earnings, he and his wife found life hard; Joseph earned extra amounts by mending furniture and teaching people to read and write. When he 5 had finished his seven years' apprenticeship, Gutteridge found work at £1 a week – a high sum that shows his skill. But very soon his employer went *bankrupt*.

'We made the last week's wages last a fortnight,' Gutteridge wrote, 'and then came the thought of where or how to find food for ourselves and our two children.' They sold their furniture piece by piece to buy bread and oatmeal for porridge. In the depths of the harshest winter they slept on bare boards, trying to keep warm without a fire. For two days they ate nothing, until someone gave them 3d (1p), enough to buy a loaf. In all this suffering he refused to ask for help from the *Poor Law*. Like other people at the time, he thought that poor relief damaged his self-respect. 'I would rather have died from sheer starvation' he wrote.

After some weeks he found work again, at 24s (£1.20) a week. With help from his employer he became a 'first hand', the most prosperous kind of weaver with his own looms at home. But earnings were still uncertain. Work was always short at Christmas, since ribbons were bought for summer clothes and were mostly made in the spring.

Gutteridge did not always work or mix easily with others. He knew that he was cleverer than most other men, including his own brothers; he had few close friends and thought of himself as one by himself because of his special interests. When you read his autobiography you get the idea that he was someone who did not laugh a great deal. He was obstinate and wrote that one 'might as well try to drive a wooden peg into an iron *anvil* as to make me *swerve* from the course of action I was resolved upon'. He was brave and tough; one evening, at the age of fifty-four, he walked across an open field, though he knew there were thieves about. He described what happened:

At the farthest end I was met by three or four men, who penned me in at the upright stones and refused to let me pass. I at once saw their object and in an instant made a straight thrust with my umbrella at the face of the fellow

6

who barred my progress. He uttered a cry of pain and left the passage free, and I hurried off in safety, thanks to a knowledge of fencing acquired in youth. The thrust went straight home and no doubt hurt the man severely.

What does that story tell you about the kind of man Gutteridge was? How would you have behaved?

Gutteridge was fierce and stern. Perhaps one reason was that he, although so clever, had to earn his living as a weaver while (as he wrote) rich men had 'the right to *dominate* over their fellow-men, who by the sweat of their brow in their *serf*-like labour' had made their employers' fortunes. Like most working men of the time, Gutteridge wanted to end these differences of wealth and power. He was a *Radical*. In Coventry, men like him at least had the advantage of working at home, rather than in factories where an employer would have been able to control every minute of their day.

2 *The Ribbon Industry*

HOW RIBBONS WERE MADE

In the eighteenth century women decorated their clothes with silk ribbons. It was at this time that Coventry weavers started to weave ribbons and in the nineteenth century they made more of them than weavers anywhere else. When Gutteridge was a baby there were 5,000 weavers in Coventry, almost one quarter of the population.

Silk comes from the *cocoons* of silkworms, which are not easy to rear in Britain. Coventry weavers tried to breed them, planting mulberry trees in their gardens since the worms fed on their leaves, but they could never get enough cocoons through this hobby; thousands of silkworms were needed to make enough silk for one length of ribbon. Silk was imported from Italy, India or China. The cocoons were boiled to remove the gum and then threads were reeled off, twisted together for weaving and dyed.

Weavers' houses had workshops for looms; these loomshops were usually upstairs. Weaving was difficult and eye-straining work; gaslight was expensive and not very bright. So the loomshops had large windows, sometimes almost filling one wall. These windows were not opened; fresh air caused moisture in the silk to evaporate, something weavers hated. (Can you think why?) The atmosphere in loomshops was thick and damp; in the winter condensation ran down the windows. So in foul air weavers worked for long hours at a stretch, in cramped positions with their chests pressed against the loom. They were often ill, being known for their pale faces and diseases of the skin and chest; many died of consumption.

8

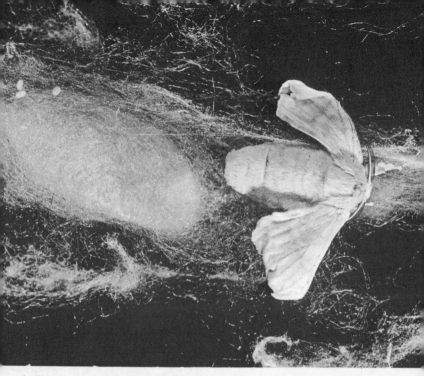

A silk moth, just emerged from its cocoon

Looms were worked by muscle power; they were called 'handlooms' but feet were used too. About 1823 a new sort of handloom, the 'Jacquard' (named after its inventor) was brought in from France to weave the most complicated and difficult patterns; Jacquards were higher than other looms and their loomshops had taller windows. Jacquard weavers were the most skilful; Joseph Gutteridge became one. Their job was dangerous; Gutteridge slipped off the top of a loom while repairing it and injured himself permanently after falling 4 metres.

Most men weavers had a few looms in their loomshops; such men were called 'first hands'. When they were counted in 1838, there were 1,800 first hands. Two hundred of these first hands were women, but most women did not own looms. First hands worked their looms with their wives, children and apprentices, or with 'journeymen' – weavers who had no looms

of their own. In Coventry, most journeymen were young weavers saving up to buy looms.

Weavers were employed by ribbon manufacturers, rich men with warehouses to store silk and finished ribbons. Weavers would collect silk from them and return with ribbons a few weeks later. Of course, manufacturers could not keep a check on silk in loomshops; they often accused weavers of stealing it. On the other hand, weavers sometimes claimed that manufacturers did not weigh silk fairly, accusing them of 'wiggling at the scale'. (What did this mean?) Another problem was that silk lost weight in the loom through evaporation. Weavers and manufacturers often had angry arguments. There were many sorts of ribbon, and weavers varied in skill, but usually a weaver could manage about 50 feet (15 m) of ribbon every week. Most looms were wide enough for weavers to make several pieces of ribbon at once – sometimes as many as twenty.

Weavers had to work for sixty hours a week to earn a living, but weaving at home they were able to choose their times of work and leisure. On Monday they often started late and finished early, but then they worked till 9 p.m. on the next four days, finishing early on Saturday. Weavers liked to take days off to visit Warwick races or the circus that often came in June to Greyfriars Green. Like many schoolchildren, they would rather work extra hard and then rest than work steadily all the time. Also, wives found it easy to weave at home, being able to go downstairs to look after the cooking and to keep young children safely near them in the loomshop.

HOW WEAVERS WERE PAID

When a weaver took his ribbons to the manufacturer's warehouse he would be paid by *piecework*; so he did not receive a weekly wage like a modern worker. Weavers wanted everyone to be paid the same for the same type of work and had long

A weaver seated at a ribbon loom. This photograph was taken in 1941 and shows one of the last Coventry weavers at work

lists of piecework rates, called 'lists of prices', which they wanted manufacturers to follow. Otherwise, weavers would never know what income to expect and would find themselves fighting each other for work. One weaver said in 1834: 'If this list is destroyed, all the *surplus* hands will be brought into immediate competition with those in work – underworking each other till we shall all be brought down to starvation level.' In fact, many manufacturers disliked competition too. (Can you say why?) They welcomed the lists. So did many shop-keepers, for if weavers' earnings fell they would have less to spend in shops. During a bad *slump* in 1818 some shopkeepers asked the manufacturers to remember that while weavers were suffering starvation, 'the *retailer* of every description is suffering in a *commensurate* degree;' they asked manufacturers not to lower earnings and so 'lash and cut the starving poor

A dress trimmed with Coventry ribbon, 1861

that dwell around you'. People used to nag at manufacturers unwilling to pay by the list – this was often successful in a small town where everybody knew each other and friends and relations passed each other in the street every day.

GROWTH OF THE RIBBON TRADE

Other countries, especially France, also made silk goods, but until 1826 the law said that foreign silks could not be imported into Britain. This meant that Coventry had the home market for ribbons almost to itself, apart from smuggled ribbons. These were a constant nuisance, because British women thought French ribbons more beautiful than Coventry's; there were stories of women coming through the Customs from France looking much fatter than usual because they had yards of ribbon wrapped round their bodies.

In 1826 Parliament tried to stop smuggling by allowing foreign goods in, but putting a *tariff* on them. The tariff was usually high enough to shelter Coventry from foreign competition and low enough to make smuggling unprofitable. Coventry manufacturers profited from the British liking for French patterns by copying them without payment. As ribbons became more and more popular, Coventry's industry boomed after 1835; the number of weavers went up from 5,000 to 11,000 between 1821 and 1861. As the price of food dropped in the 1850s ordinary people could afford to buy more luxuries like ribbons. 'From the low price of provisions', someone wrote in 1852, '*multitudes* have something more to spare from their weekly wages than formerly, for the purchase of finery: and the demand for cheap ribbons has increased wonderfully.'

Opposite: *A Coventry ribbon woven for the Great Exhibition, 1851*   15

3 Other Outwork Industries

When Joseph Gutteridge was a weaver, many things besides silk ribbons were made in people's homes, not in factories. For example, a lot of cloth was woven in houses – cotton in Lancashire, wool in Yorkshire, Somerset and Wales, silk in Spitalfields (in London). Nails were made by men, women and children in the Black Country, west of Birmingham. Lace was made in Nottingham, and stockings in Leicester. Boots and shoes were made in houses in Northamptonshire. These are just a few examples of 'outwork'.

LONDON CLOTHING WORKERS AND TOYMAKERS

Most clothes were made by outwork. We know how these outworkers lived because a *journalist* called Henry Mayhew wrote long articles about them in a newspaper in 1849 and 1850. He told of one man in London who sewed trousers for soldiers' uniforms, living and working in one room. He sewed one pair every six hours. For this work he was paid 6*d* (2½p); so, working eighty hours a week, he made sixteen pairs of trousers and earned 8*s* (40p). But after buying thread and paying someone to take finished trousers to his employer and bring back cloth, he was left with less than half his earnings. To make ends meet he took in four lodgers, but when Mayhew saw him two of them were unemployed and owed him money. The trouser-sewer had been forced to *pawn* most of his bed-clothes and his lodgers' sheets hadn't been changed for three months. His own shirt hadn't been changed for a month. Food for his cat cost 3½*d* (1½p) a week – half the price of a 4lb (2 kg)

16

Making nails in the Black Country, near Birmingham, about 1890. The girl is pointing nails, using two hammers, one in her hand and a mechanical hammer, or 'oliver', worked with her feet

loaf and more than he could afford. His pet canary he called an 'extravagance'.

Mayhew also visited a widow aged more than seventy who lived in one small room and sewed convicts' uniforms. For each uniform (jacket, trousers and waistcoat) needing one-and-a-half days' work she was paid 7¾d (3p). A full week's work brought 3s (15p). Mayhew wrote:

There was no table in the room; but on a chair without a back there was an old tin tray, on which stood a cup of 17 hot, milkless tea, and a broken saucer, with some half dozen small potatoes in it. It was the poor soul's dinner. Some tea-leaves had been given her and she had boiled them up again to make something like a meal. She had not even a morsel of bread. In one corner of the room was a hay mattress, rolled up. With this she slept on the floor.

She had no coat and felt the cold keenly. The week before Mayhew's visit she had sold a cup and saucer so as to buy a candle. The Poor Law refused her relief because she was still fit enough to work.

Mayhew also wrote about many toymakers in London. One made wooden toys in his workshop at home and Mayhew wrote: 'Toys were piled all over the workshop. It was not very easy for a stranger to stir without the risk of upsetting a long line of *omnibuses* or wrecking a perfect fleet of steamboats.' The toymaker carved parts of a toy with a knife and then glued them together and painted them. Some years before Mayhew spoke to him (in 1850), his most common toys were spotted horses on wheels, but these had gone out of fashion. He was making steamboats instead but they did not sell as well. As he said to Mayhew: 'Every child has seen a horse, but there's numbers never see a steamboat and so care nothing about them.' He also made 'scratchbacks' – toys which 'frolicsome people', as he called them, rubbed on friends' backs to startle them with a whirring sound.

His toys were sold for 1*d* ($\frac{1}{2}$p) to poor children, often the children of the Spitalfields silk weavers who lived nearby. When weavers were badly off, the toy trade slumped. Still, he earned about £1 a week – far more than the clothes makers. Another man making moving models of cats, elephants and pigs from wood and *papier maché* earned about the same. He was very skilful and invented the arrangements of wheels and wire that moved his toys; his elephants moved their tails as well as their trunks. He complained that no toymaker was really well paid for his work and cleverness. Still, he earned far more than some women seen by Mayhew, who made

A family of silkworkers in Spitalfields, 1861. They are working late into the evening, as the new moon shows. Notice the silk bobbins, birdcage and sleeping children. The girl on the left is winding silk onto bobbins

papier maché animals and covered them with rabbit fur – unpleasant work because the fur stank. They earned between 4*s* (20p) and 11*s* (55p) a week.

Mayhew found that outworkers' earnings depended on whether they had a trade union to protect them and on how many workers were competing against each other for jobs. Women always earned less than men. They did not have trade unions and there were always too many women for the work available. Widows needed jobs desperately and so were paid very little. Mayhew also found that when goods came in from abroad wages in Britain were lower; the women toy-makers' wages were kept down by cheap toy rabbits and dogs from Germany.

BEDFORDSHIRE STRAW PLAITERS AND HATTERS

Another example of outwork comes from Bedfordshire. Straw was *plaited* in strips; the plaits were used to make hats. Most plaiters were women and children; there were over 20,000 of them. Plaiters bought straw in the market, in bundles about six inches (150 mm) across, and took the plaited straw back to the market to sell it. Like silkweaving, plaiting made your eyes tired, but plaiters did not have specially large windows in their cottages; they placed glass bottles round candles so as to increase the light. (How does this happen?)

Children were often sent to plaiting 'schools', where they learnt very little and plaited a lot. These schools were really workshops and the teachers really forewomen. Pupils brought straw from home and the teacher forced them to plait it, sometimes caning them when they were slow. The youngest plaiter we know about was two; many were as young as seven or eight. Sometimes children were expected to plait seventeen yards (15 m) a day and the school day might last as long as ten hours.

Children at plaiting school suffered from catarrh and stomach troubles through working long hours in overcrowded and stuffy classrooms. Their lips got sore too, because of the habit of moistening straws in the mouth to keep them flexible. Children found plaiting terribly boring; one boy said that farm work was better, because 'you could lie down while your sheep and things was eating'.

Plaited straw was taken from Bedfordshire villages into the nearby towns of Dunstable and Luton. There, it was made into women's hats. In Luton hundreds of houses were specially built for outworkers, with two large rooms at the back. Hats

Opposite: *An engraving of 1861 showing scenes in the life of straw plaiters from Dunstable, Bedfordshire*

Buying Cut Straw.

Selling Plait.

Plaiting School.

A Plaiter's Home.

A photograph taken in the 1960s shows a woman making nets in Burton Bradstock, Dorset, as they were made in Victorian times

were wanted in the spring (like silk ribbons) when women bought their new clothes; so the hatmakers worked very long hours from February to May and had little to do with straw the rest of the year. Most hatmakers were women and children; the youngest we know about was four years old.

It was hard to combine housework with sewing hats. Housewives busy sewing all day got girls of thirteen or fourteen to look after their young children and sent their dirty clothes to a neighbour's house to be washed. One writer described seeing two children ill with measles in cradles in a hatter's kitchen, while other children were busy sewing upstairs amid unmade beds and hats were piling up in the parlour.

DORSET NETS AND BUTTONS

Other examples of outwork come from Dorset, a long way to the south-west of Bedfordshire. In the villages round Bridport

Opposite: *Making straw hats, a painting of 1891 shows Bedfordshire hatmakers at work*

women made nets for fishing, tennis, billiard-tables, hammocks and catching rabbits. Dorset nets went all over the world – for example, to the fishing boats in Newfoundland. The work of making nets was called 'braiding'. The *twine* came from mills in Bridport and was brought out by carts to the villages.

A Dorset button. Notice how the thread is wound over a wire frame

Nets were too big to fit easily into cottages; the braiders liked to work in the open air, spreading the nets on the ground and hanging one end on a hook in the cottage wall.

Braiding was taught by mothers to their daughters. Unlike straw plaiting, it was not taught in schools, perhaps because the nets were too big for classrooms. Dorset mothers grumbled

24

about schools because they took their girls away from useful work.

Buttons for shirts and dresses were also made in Dorset, mostly in the little town of Shaftesbury. The buttons had a wire frame. The wire came in bundles from Birmingham. Children bent pieces of wire into rings and then soldered the ends together. Women then covered the hole in the middle with thread and embroidered it in fancy patterns, filling the hole to make the button. A really expert sewer could make eighty buttons in a day. For this she would get no more than 2s (10p). Children got 1s (5p) a week. Finally, the buttons were sewn onto cards for shops. This is still done to buttons today though they are made in a quite different way.

Britain had many different kinds of outworkers; most of them were very poor, but some better off, such as Coventry weavers like Gutteridge.

4 *Home Life*

In Coventry, some weavers earned very little and others quite a lot. Women who wound silk onto bobbins ready for weaving were paid only 5s (25p) a week. Men and women working on looms received more; journeymen (and women) earned about 10s (50p) a week and first hands about 12s (60p). Very skilful weavers (like Gutteridge) were paid more.

Often weavers' wives wove too and this meant that family earnings were higher. A first hand with four looms worked by his family earned over £2 a week or eight times as much as the poorest ribbon workers.

The poorest weavers had very little furniture. Their beds were sacks of straw resting on bricks, with no sheets. Someone described the diet of such a family in 1863:

> BREAKFAST Children have bread and treacle; adults have tea or coffee and bread with lettuce perhaps.
> DINNER Bacon and potatoes; and in this case the bacon and potatoes are boiled together and the water is thrown away. [The potatoes were boiled in their jackets and the skins eaten.]
> TEA Tea and bread.
> SUPPER Bread and cheese.

Weavers always spent a lot of their money on bread, potatoes and bacon. They were cheap and did not take long to cook.

This was important, because wives worked long hours and could not spare the time to cook complicated meals, even when they were working at home. Weavers ate little during the day, merely taking a snack at the loom. The main meal was in the evening.

The very poorest people lived on a few pence a week. Elizabeth Whiting was a widow with four young children. She made brushes in her house in Kenton Street, London, and earned between 3s (15p) and 5s (25p) a week. She paid 3s (15p) a week rent, but sometimes had to owe it for weeks. This was how she spent her money in the week beginning 15 December 1839:

SUNDAY: Bought on Saturday night – potatoes 1½d [½p], bacon 2d [1p], candle ½d, tea and sugar 2d [1p], soap 1½d [½p], coals 2d [1p], loaf 8½d [3p]	1s 6d	[7½p]
MONDAY: Tea and sugar 2d, butter 1½d, candle ½d	4d	[2p]
TUESDAY: Coals	2d	[1p]
WEDNESDAY: Tea and sugar 2d, candle ½d, wood ½d, potatoes 1d	4d	[2p]
THURSDAY: Coals	1d	[½p]
FRIDAY and SATURDAY	—	
	2s 5d	[12p]

In addition, five 4 lb (2 kg) loaves were given by the Poor Law; without them the family might have starved. Elizabeth Whiting bought goods in tiny amounts. In this week her family lived on 24 lbs (11 kg) of bread, 5 lbs (2¼ kg) of potatoes, 5 oz (145 g) of bacon and 1 oz (30 g) of tea. Tea was their one luxury; the leaves were used twice. Five pence (2p) bought 100 lbs (45 kg) of coal; a fire was essential in the winter not only for warmth but also to cook on.

Families earning 30s (£1.50) a week were much better off. 27

Here is the weekly budget of one such family, with five children:

2 oz tea [55 g]		8d	[3p]
7 oz coffee [200 g]		10½d	[4½p]
3 lb sugar [1½ kg]	1s	9d	[9p]
1 cwt coal [50 kg]; also coke and wood	2s	3d	[11p]
12 loaves at 8d each	8s	0d	[40p]
18 lb potatoes [8 kg]		9d	[4p]
1½ lb butter [¾ kg]	1s	6d	[7½p]
1 lb soap [½ kg], ½ lb soda [¼ kg]		7d	[3p]
blue and starch (for ironing clothes)		2d	[1p]
1 lb candles [½ kg]		7d	[3p]
5 lb bacon [2¼ kg]	2s	6d	[12½p]
greens or turnips, onions etc.		6d	[2½p]
pepper, salt and mustard		3d	[1p]
herrings		9d	[4p]
snuff		6d	[2½p]
7 lb meat [3 kg]	3s	6d	[17½p]
rent	4s	0d	[20p]
	£1 9s	1½d	[£1 45½p]

Compared to most working people, this family lived well, eating meat every day. *Snuff*, coffee and tea were luxuries. Notice that tea cost 27p a lb (½ kg) – almost a third of what it costs today, though wages have risen at least fifty times since the 1840s. The family had only a few pence over from £1.50

Opposite: *The living room of a worker's house in about 1860. 20 Castle Street (see page 30) would look like this inside. Compared with most Victorian working people this family is well fed and clothed and has good furniture, though there is no carpet on the wooden floor. There is a cast iron cooker in the fireplace, and also a hook to hang stewpots on above the fire. The room is lit by gas, and the woman has a candle for close work; notice the candle snuffer and the needle case*

a week for clothes and children's school fees. A rise in the price of basic foods such as bread and potatoes meant hardship for even better-off families and hunger for the very poor, who spent more than half their income on them. In 1847 the price of a 4 lb (2 kg) loaf rose to $11\frac{1}{2}d$ (5p) – a desperately high price for Elizabeth Whiting and people like her. Fortunately, the price of bread dropped again by 1850.

HOUSES

The plan shows a first hand weaver's house, 20 Castle Street, Hillfields, in Coventry, built in the 1830s when Gutteridge was an apprentice. The rent of a house like the one illustrated was between $3s$ (15p) and $4s$ (20p) a week. Work out what percentage of a first hand's earnings that was. Compare it with the rents of modern houses.

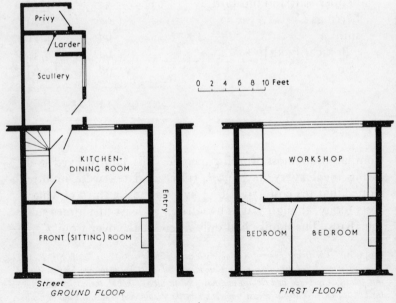

20 Castle Street, Hillfields: a two story weaver's house.

Measure the house with the scale in the plan. Compare the size and number of rooms with those in your house. Today houses are not built with only two bedrooms, like 20 Castle Street and thousands of cottages like it. Living in such houses weavers with large families like Gutteridge found they were very crowded. Bedroom space was short and children often slept downstairs. Even so, the family living in 20 Castle Street was better-off than many working people of the day; for example, most farm labourers' cottages were smaller still and did not have a separate parlour.

Notice that the loomshop takes as much space as the two bedrooms. A loomshop this size held two looms, the average number for first hands. Men with more looms rented a house with three storeys; the loomshop filled the top floor.

5 Town Life

POVERTY

In 1856 a Coventry clergyman wrote in his diary:

> This day I visited a woman in a dying state. She had been
> fifteen months married. Her husband is an apprentice at
> 4s [20p] per week. She worked in a factory; she has not
> been able to work for nearly three months. The doctor
> says that she cannot live more than two days. Her condition
> is painfully interesting. She is in lodgings at 2s 6d [12½p]
> a week. The neighbours say that both she and her husband
> are in a state bordering on starvation. I talked to her of
> heaven and the way to prepare for it. The tears rolled
> silently down her pale cheeks. . .

In Victorian towns there were always some people as poor as
this. There were never enough jobs to go round, and the ill
and the very old could not work anyway. The very poor could
not afford houses of their own. One Coventry writer tells of
their living:

> cooped together in a space too small for the same number
> of cattle, a dozen or a score of families having one common
> yard, or space of ground. . . Rooms in such houses are
> generally let furnished; the furniture consisting of a
> miserable bed, two or three old chairs, an old table and a
> few cooking utensils. Some of these rooms are the day and
> night residence of seven or even ten persons. At night the
> clothing of the one miserable *pallet* is divided into two or
> three shares. . . and forms the resting place of many a

haggard countenance and of limbs perished through cold through the severity of the winter season.

Most weavers were much better-off than this, but they might suddenly become unemployed and poor. Every few years there was a large slump. In Gutteridge's lifetime, the two worst were in 1829–33 and 1860–63. The first of these began when Gutteridge was thirteen and recently apprenticed in the ribbon trade. Shops could not sell ribbons. Many weavers had no work. Manufacturers tried to boost sales by cutting prices. They reduced the list of prices several times and sometimes dropped it altogether.

Joseph Gutteridge recalled this time in his autobiography written more than sixty years later:

> About this time we had long intervals without employment, and some of our experiences were bitter indeed, particularly in the severe winter, with bread at famine prices and potatoes spoiled by the frost so as to be almost uneatable.
>
> These were times of suffering not easily forgotten. My father had been out of work about sixteen weeks, and we lads were earning but little and scarcely knew where to look for the means to satisfy our hunger. One day on coming home I picked up from a heap of rubbish a piece of paper, which was at once recognised to be a One Pound note. I hurried home gleefully with my prize, thinking it would be received with delight as a means of buying food, or at least paying for what we had already had on *credit* from a little shop in the neighbourhood. My father sent me and a brother to the shop, not however to pay off the old score, but to *solicit* credit for another week's provisions. When the shopkeeper heard our appeal, told in language that only hungry lads could use, he filled our basket and bade us come again for what we wanted until times improved. This was just before Christmas and on Christmas Eve the shopkeeper sent us as a present some grocery and

a quart [1 litre] of home-brewed ale with which to keep the festival. The One Pound note was not claimed by anyone, although we had made it well known that we had found it. It was kept for three weeks and was then handed over to the shopkeeper who had so kindly befriended us in our time of need.

Why did Gutteridge's father not spend the pound note on food?

In times like these, most unemployed weavers were much less lucky than Gutteridge's family on this occasion. They would get enough to keep them alive, but not much more, from the Poor Law or from special relief funds collected by better-off people in Coventry. So in 1841 and 1842 £2,300 was collected and spent on 72,000 loaves for the poor. One man said: 'It added in no small degree to the beauty of the landscape and formed a bond of union between the parties, when those who were in *affluent* circumstances felt disposed to assist those who stood in need. . . .' What did he mean by 'the beauty of the landscape' and 'a bond of union between the parties'?

HELPING EACH OTHER

At the end of 1844 one of Gutteridge's sons died of smallpox. Gutteridge was in despair because he was unemployed and could not pay for the funeral. A collection among friends at a New Year dance provided the money. Help like this made Gutteridge see, like many other working men, that they could improve their lives by banding together to assist each other. Doing this was often called 'self-help'. This meant working people helping themselves, rather than relying on the charity of richer persons. So Gutteridge joined a *friendly society*, the 'Oddfellows', paying a few pence into its fund every week. In return, the society kept his family from starving by paying him 10s (50p) a week one winter when he was seriously ill and unable to work.

The first friendly societies began in the seventeenth century. After 1800 they grew quickly. They were counted in 1872.

The top of a letter giving permission (dispensation) to begin another branch of the Oddfellows Friendly Society. The sun and other symbols have been used by the society since it began. What do they stand for?

Four million people, about one person in seven, were members of friendly societies; over 400,000 were in the biggest, the Unity of Oddfellows, which had branches all over the country, including the one at Coventry that Gutteridge joined. Most societies were small, with fewer than a hundred members and only one branch. Counting these one-branch societies, as well as the big societies with many branches, there were 32,000 branches altogether, sixty of them in Coventry.

Friendly societies helped members in the ways that the 'Welfare State' does now. In return for a subscription, members received payments when they were ill or when a relative died. Sometimes societies paid doctors to visit sick members, or gave pensions to members too old to work. Unless they joined friendly societies working people could get such help only from charity or the Poor Law, which they hated. One Odd-fellow called workhouses 'barracks for lodging *paupers*, by which means the working man has been taught to look upon himself as a "thing" depending on others, rather than as a 35

being whose labour and industrious habits added *dignity* to his position in society'. In contrast, friendly societies helped people to keep their self-respect.

Friendly societies were run wholly by working people. Members elected the *chairman* and secretary of the branch and collected subscriptions. Each branch usually met once a month in a public house, and after the society's business there was a party, with songs like 'Hearts of Oak' (about the navy) and 'The Roast Beef of Old England'.

One of the most important sorts of 'self-help' was for working people to have shops and share the profits. They were called co-operative shops. They began in the 1820s. For the rest of the century the numbers of them grew and by 1900 every town had one.

Coventry's co-operative shop began in 1867. Some weavers and others decided that it would help to make poor people happier by saving money. So they founded the Coventry Perseverance Co-operative Society. Forty-eight members soon joined and a small grocery shop was opened in Cook Street. At first members served in the shop. Takings in the first week were 8s 9½d (44p). The first *dividend* was 5 per cent. By 1900 the society grew to have a dozen shops and 5,000 members, and paid a dividend of 12½ per cent. This meant that members were only paying 87½p for food and clothes that in other shops cost £1. But co-operative societies would not give credit. People like Gutteridge liked co-operative shops; they hated credit, because it got you into debt that was hard to repay. People who found it impossible to live without credit could not join the 'co-op'. Why did this mean that the very poorest sometimes could not join?

Like workers in other industries, the Coventry ribbon weavers helped themselves by forming a trade union. Trade unions were banned by law till 1824. After then, attempts to start a weavers' union in Coventry did not succeed until 1842

Opposite: *The first co-operative shop in Coventry, photographed about 1917. Notice the clothes in the shop window, and the footscrapers, window shutters and cobbled street*

when most of the weavers in the city joined it, as Joseph Gutteridge did. Even so, by our standards it was a small union, for only one town. In other industries employers did their best to stamp out trade unions, refusing to bargain with them over wages and sacking union members. The Coventry ribbon manufacturers, however, usually worked well with the union in keeping up the list of prices, because they did not want their rivals to be able to sell cheaper ribbons than theirs. For its part the union did not often call strikes; in any case it did not have enough money for strike pay. The union's motto was, 'The interests of masters and workpeople are one, where honour presides.' (What does this mean?) But there were many small quarrels between masters and weavers, usually over the quality and weight of ribbons. Why did quarrels arise easily over these? Masters or weavers often took their quarrels to the law courts, and the union had a lawyer to defend their cases in court. One of the most important battles took place in 1850, when he got the magistrates to agree that factory owners had by law to give their employees (working from 7 a.m. to 6.30 in the evening with just a one-hour break) an extra half-hour for breakfast.

OVERCROWDING, DIRT AND DISEASE

In the 1820s, when Gutteridge was a boy, Coventry, like most Victorian towns, was by our standards a small place. It was nowhere more than $1\frac{1}{2}$ kilometres across, and the fields where he collected flowers were a short walk from home. Though the population was growing, the town could not spread out very far; people had the right to graze cows and horses on fields near the town, and so stopped the owners selling the fields for building. This 'grazing right' started in the Middle Ages when many townspeople had cattle. By the nineteenth century only two or three hundred townspeople had cattle,

Opposite: *Greyfriars Green, Coventry, an engraving from about 1850. Where the sheep grazed, there is now an urban motorway. Coventry was often called 'the city of three spires'. Notice the ribbon factory, near the church on the left*

most of them being butchers, but the town was still gripped tight in a ring of fields.

Many Coventry streets were so narrow that two carts could not pass one another. Black and white houses built in the Middle Ages overhung the street; and because of the shortage of land on the edge of the town their gardens were sold for building. Houses were built on them in squares with courtyards in the middle; they could only be reached from the street by narrow passages between the original houses. So many parts of the city were very overcrowded, houses being jumbled up tightly together. Palmer Lane, for example, was described as 'one entire mass of old rubbishy houses, scarcely one of which ought to be inhabited by human beings and yet all are densely occupied by very poor people'.

When Gutteridge was a boy, he used to play on Primrose Hill, just north of the town. As an old man he remembered it as 'a most romantic, wild and beautiful place', where primroses and daffodils covered the ground and tall elm trees grew in an old quarry. But when he was ten years old many weavers' houses were built there, making the new suburb of Hillfields. The houses were given more space than in the old parts of town, but the roads were not paved or drained, and the primroses were replaced by deep pools of mud. In wet weather carts sank up to their axles.

Instead of water closets Coventry houses had *privies* opening into cesspits; smaller houses shared privies and in some parts of town there was one for as many as seventeen houses. Men came round with carts and shovels to clean out the cesspits. Often they left the filth piled up in the street. This was why, for example, there was in Harnall Lane in 1849 what one man called 'an immense heap of soil, *impregnated* with the *debris* of an adjoining stable and cowhouse'. The heap stretched two-thirds of the way across the street. Lots more dirt in Coventry came from pigs; people kept them for meat, feeding them on scraps.

Much dirt was washed downhill into the Sherbourne, a
black and filthy river. It flowed slowly because there were

The corner of Broadgate and Smithford Street, Coventry, photographed in 1859. A top-halled policeman stands in the middle of Broadgate. Notice the head of Peeping Tom, on the corner of Smithford Street and Hertford Street

three *mill-dams* across it. One man calculated that 9,000 tonnes of dirt lay piled behind them. In winter the river sometimes flooded Spon Street, covering the ground floor of houses with 75 millimetres of stinking mud.

41

Most people got their water from wells. They worked a pump with a long handle to raise water from the bottom of the well and took it home in wooden buckets. About 500 houses, out of 7,000 in the city, had water piped from two small waterworks. This did not mean the regular supply that we take for granted, since the pipes were too narrow to carry enough water and people sometimes found themselves without water for days.

Like most British towns Coventry was very unhealthy because of dirt and polluted water. Every year in Coventry 26 people out of every 1,000 died. (Today about 12 in every 1,000 die.) There were many *epidemics* of killing diseases – for example an outbreak of *cholera* in 1849. It was caused by *microbes* in impure water and broke out first in houses in Harnall Lane, near the heap of filth mentioned on page 40.

People who caught cholera had continuous diarrhoea which caused *dehydration* and usually led to death. In July, August and September 1849 over two hundred people died of cholera in Coventry.

No one had ever bothered about public health in Coventry. The cholera epidemic made people realise that dirt meant death. At the same time a new Act of Parliament, the Public Health Act, forced the town council to clean up the city. So in the 1850s the council, like councils in other British towns, began to put in water-closets and to build sewers. A large waterworks was built and water was piped from it to city houses. The Sherbourne was cleaned out and the mill-dams removed. In 1857 the new main sewer was completed and it started to put sewage into the Sherbourne below the town. Very soon there were complaints from Stratford-on-Avon that Coventry was polluting the river – something that reminds us that we cannot plan the health of one town, or write its history, without thinking of other places too.

Also in the 1850s, the grazing rights were ended. Very soon the fields round the town were covered with houses. But the last privies were not replaced till the 1920s and the last court-yard houses not till the 1960s.

6 Leisure

The most important holiday in Coventry took place in June when the Great Fair and procession were held. The procession was over a kilometre long and took five hours to parade through the town. Many inhabitants took time off work to watch it.

The chief member of the procession was 'Lady Godiva', remembering the famous ancient legend about the countess who is said to have ridden through the city naked in the eleventh century as an act of sacrifice to get taxes removed. However, the actress who now played the part was not naked, but clothed from head to foot in very unrevealing clothes; sometimes she even wore a huge hat with feathers and carried an umbrella. From time to time there was a Peeping Tom too; he was carried inside a wooden shed on top of a waggon and popped his head out of the window to joke with the crowd.

Also in the parade was a very odd mixture of people, most of them having nothing to do with Lady Godiva. There was St George, the White Knight, the Red Cross Knight, Robin Hood and Friar Tuck, and indeed any other quaint figures for whom the organisers could get actors and costumes. In 1848 an elephant was brought to Coventry by Wombwell's Circus as part of the Great Fair fun; so he was placed at the head of the parade with a wooden castle on his back as 'a living representation' of the city's coat of arms. Once, Lady Godiva was dropped altogether from the procession – in 1832, just after the Great Reform Act; instead, the place of honour

43

went to the Champion of Reform mounted on a white horse and carrying the Reform Act.

There were always several bands in the procession, one of them consisting of soldiers from the barracks, and there were also old men dressed up as the City Guards in medieval armour; a newspaper said about them in 1842 that they were 'a parcel of poor decrepit old men, upon whom the remains of ancient armour produced a most *ludicrous* appearance'. Young children came as 'followers' for Lady Godiva; there was always great competition among people in the town to get their children into the procession and some of them were so small that they had to be strapped into basket seats on their horses to stop them falling off. Men from the city's trades also paraded, with banners like that of the silk dyers: 'We dye to live and live to die.' Friendly societies marched or rode too, like Gutteridge's Oddfellows, though he does not seem to have been with them.

The crowds enjoying the procession got bigger year by year when Gutteridge was in his twenties and thirties, as the new railways made it possible to travel a long way to see it. By the 1840s thousands were coming by special trains from all over the Midlands. After the parade they stayed to enjoy amusements that lasted for days, making the only big holiday in the year apart from Christmas. There were conjurors, coconut shies and contests to climb a pole covered with grease. The biggest attraction was the circus; besides the thrills we know today, it gave people the only real chance they had to see what elephants and lions looked like, at a time when no one had films or TV or even many books with pictures.

Some people disliked the Great Fair. It was very noisy; in 1859 someone living near the field where the fair was held complained that he was disturbed all day by drums, bagpipes, monkeys, parrots, a bear and a barrel organ playing 'Annie Laurie'. He was also woken up by a cock crowing at 3 a.m.

Opposite: *A painting of the start of the Godiva procession, 1867. Notice Lady Godiva on her horse, the banners, the band, the infant 'follower', and St George*

People were disgusted by the drunkenness at the procession and fair. In 1844 Lady Godiva herself was drunk and swayed about on her horse. A Coventry clergyman, Thomas Collins, called for the banning of the 'old, bad, *lewd*, Lady Godiva custom'. In reply, supporters of the procession burnt a full-scale model of him in the street. The next procession was drenched with rain and had to be ended early. Some said that Mr Collins's prayers brought the downpour.

PUBLIC HANGINGS

Almost as popular as the Great Fair were the public hangings of murderers. These hangings took place every two or three years and remind us that life in Victorian towns was brutal. In 1831, when Gutteridge was fifteen, Mary Ann Higgins was hanged. She was nineteen years old and was sentenced to death for poisoning her uncle to get a few pounds so that she could afford to get married. The real villain was her lover, but he was careful to send her into the chemist's shop to buy the arsenic and so was acquitted for lack of evidence.

On the day of execution Mary Higgins was taken from the gaol to the gallows on Whitley Common sitting in a cart on her coffin. Fifteen thousand spectators watched her being hanged; among them was her lover. As her body hung on the gallows twenty women with *goitres* came forward to rub her right hand against them; it was a *superstition* that this would cure them. Later, her body was taken back to the gaol and put on exhibition for a few days. Parents brought their children to see it. Murderers were hanged in public in Britain till 1868.

THE PLEASURES OF SCIENCE

Gutteridge was not interested in the Great Fair and thought public hangings disgusting. His pleasure came from science and making things. These hobbies gave him happiness – unlike weaving which was *monotonous* work and made little use of his brain.

He was very clever at making things – even the tools he used in his carpentry. He made a tenon saw from a steel corset-stay and chisels from worn-out files given to him by friends. He covered all the flat surfaces of the furniture at home with wooden *mosaics* to decorate them.

One of the things he most liked doing was making violins. He made his first when he was twenty, but he was not pleased with its musical tone and threw it away. Learning the art of violin-making meant years of patient effort, copying instruments whose tone he liked. When a dealer tried to sell him a polished but screechy violin, made cheaply by machinery 'simply to sell', Gutteridge was disgusted. He carefully copied an Italian violin, using for the back a block of English maple he picked up in a timber-yard. Another violin he made from an old walnut table-top and some pine from an old loom. His violins became famous. One man even wrote from Australia to try to buy them. But though Gutteridge was short of money at the time he refused to sell them. 'They seemed', he wrote, 'like household treasures, and to send them thousands of miles away would be almost like parting with my own children.'

Gutteridge was fascinated by electricity – a great Victorian discovery. He made electrical machines, including one that he hoped would cure diseases by giving people mild shocks. He also made a *kaleidoscope* and several microscopes, the most difficult task of all because his work had to be so fine and delicate.

Throughout his life he continued his early love for nature. Gutteridge made large collections of fossils, corals and shells. He took every chance of picking up specimens, visiting nearby colliery spoil-heaps for fossils. Friends sent him thousands of shells from all over the world. Gutteridge laid out his parlour as a 'museum' and made glass cases to hold his collections. Many visitors came to see the museum that filled the tiny parlour.

Like most Victorians, Gutteridge was brought up to believe in God; and with many others he came as a man to doubt whether there was a God and went through misery because of his doubt. He wrote of 'the fearful *ordeal* of a young and ardent life wasted in the cold chilling atmosphere of unbelief'.

Science helped to remove the doubts and to make Gutteridge happier, since it proved to him that the universe was so well organised that it must have been planned by somebody.

A kaleidoscope and its box. The discs are filled with chips of rock and crystal. A disc is placed in the right-hand end of the kaleidoscope; the eyepiece is on the left. Mirrors inside make patterns with the disc, which change when the black part of the barrel is twisted and the chips move about

Most weavers were not keen on these sorts of things, but Gutteridge had a few close friends who were. They formed a 'mutual improvement society' to talk about their hobbies. At one meeting Gutteridge gave a talk on 'The *Physiology* of Digestion'. Members also recited poetry and drank tea or cocoa: they disapproved of alcohol because it made people drunk. There were seven such societies in Coventry with two hundred members altogether, about 1 per cent of the city's adult population. There were similar societies in other towns.

7 The Coming of Steam

Silk was a delicate thread that easily broke in the loom. For this reason it was very hard to run a silk loom with steam power; the extra speed snapped the thread. The problem was not solved till the 1830s, fifty years after steam looms were first used in cotton weaving. As late as 1838 there were only fifty steam looms in Coventry. But afterwards, especially in the 1850s, the number grew rapidly; by 1860 there were 1,500 steam looms in large factories.

Weavers hated factories. They split up families; husbands and wives could not usually work side by side in them, and mothers were certainly not able to take young children to work. They had to leave them at home, where from time to time they suffered dreadful accidents which weavers complained of at their trade union meetings. One occurred in 1855. Two children, aged three and six, were left alone in the morning when their parents departed for the factory, locking the house to try to keep them safe. The elder child dressed the other; neighbours heard them singing a hymn together. Then the kettle boiled over on the *hob* and the elder child's clothes caught fire when he went to rescue it. He was burned to death as neighbours were unable to reach him.

In factories, weavers could not work when they chose. If they took days off they were dismissed. Machines were working at the same time for everybody and all workers had breaks together. Weavers hated the factory rules because they were used to the freedom of the outdoor system; they especially disliked the foremen whose job it was to keep weavers con-

stantly at work. One weaver complained: 'He had heard that at one factory, a man had been paid to walk up and down, to see that each of the men were constantly at work, for which he received so much per loom; such a system was *degrading* to Englishmen and he wanted to see the time when men will not, for the sake of hire, accept such a slave master's post.'

He spoke these words in 1858, when British people were talking about black slavery in the United States. To call a foreman a 'slave master' was to say that factories were brutal and cruel places. Factory weavers wanted the same freedom as the outdoor weavers. James Hart, the owner of the largest factory, expected his weavers to make 6 yards ($5\frac{1}{2}$ m) a day each. If you compare this amount with the figure for hand-looms given on page 11, you will see how much faster steam looms were. A few weavers refused his order, making only 10 inches (25 cm) a day and spending much of the time playing cards, reading newspapers and even playing cricket along the gangways between the looms. Hart prosecuted seventeen weavers for *breach of contract*.

Factory weavers were paid weekly wages, not by piecework. Steam looms were so fast that if weavers had been paid by the list of prices they would have earned very high wages.

COTTAGE FACTORIES

Factories made ribbons more cheaply than the handlooms of the outdoor weavers. If handloom weavers did not manage to compete with steam looms they would be forced out of business. So, in 1855, outdoor weavers began to buy a much bigger and faster handloom, the 'à la bar' loom. These looms cost £34, or about eight months earnings for a very skilful weaver; the price equals about £2,500 in today's wages. Weavers formed a club, the 'A La Bar Loom Society', to help each other to buy the looms in easy instalments. It worked rather like a *building society* today. It lent weavers the full

The Kingfield cottage factories. The topshops are very high, to make room for tall Jacquard looms; the windows almost fill the wall, to admit as much light as possible

price, which they repaid at 3*s* (15p) a week. How long would repayment take?

A la bar looms were too big to be worked by weavers' muscle power; they hired 'turning boys' aged twelve or thirteen, to work the bar that kept the loom moving. An even better plan was to fit steam engines to cottages – and Coventry became the only city in the world to build 'cottage factories'. Steam engines were placed in sheds at the ends of terraces of houses and shafting for steam power was run through the workshops, for each first hand to link up to his looms with a belt. The grandest cottage factories were built in 1856 in Kingfield. A weavers' newspaper said that they combined 'all the advantages of the factory with the comfort of the private house and the domestic hearth'. By 1860 there were 1,000 steam looms in cottage factories.

By 1858 the outdoor weavers decided that the only way to beat the steam factories was to raise their costs, by forcing the factories to pay their weavers by the list of prices instead of weekly wages. Factory weavers wanted to be paid by the list too; it would raise their earnings. To explain their demands the weavers' trade union printed a notice and stuck it on walls throughout the city. It said that weavers realised that 'unless the prices paid out of doors...could be established in the factories', the result would be 'most *disastrous* to the whole weaving community'.

In the summer bands of weavers went to see the factory masters to demand 'the list'. One group went to see William Andrews, the manager of the Cash brothers' weaving business. Andrews' diary tells us what happened. The weavers visited him twice in June, but Andrews refused to pay by the list:

> JULY 2: A final *deputation* wait on me this morning to know if I will sign the list. I *decline*. They threaten that they will have a meeting at St Mary's Hall. They had a paper signed by most of my hands – 'That we are of opinion that the conduct of Mr Andrews as reported by the deputation that have waited on him is most *despicable*, and we are determined to use every means,' etc., etc.,
>
> JULY 6: Mr John Cash insists I hold out saying that if I cannot, he will shut up the business.

Two weeks later the weavers came again. Andrews said 'No' once more. Then the weavers went to see the Cash brothers, Joseph and John, pointing out that a strike might ruin them. Soon after, Andrews wrote in his diary: 'Mr John decides that I am to sign the list. It is much to my annoyance as it was by their advice I refused at first.'

In the summer weavers visited all the factory masters, one by one. Most gave in, like the Cash brothers. To celebrate, 6,000 weavers paraded through the city on 23 August with banners and bands.

53

But six factory masters would not surrender. They said that they could not meet foreign competition if their costs were raised and they threatened to *lock out* their weavers. In reply, the weavers condemned the '*brutalising* slavery of the "Bunch of Six"': 'Yes, their wives and daughters walk about in jewellery and gold, while they retire in the prime of life upon *colossal* fortunes.' A lock-out began on Saturday 4 September; 1,000 weavers were thrown out of work. The other weavers still at work paid one-sixth of their earnings into a fund for the 'lock-outs'.

Many people in Coventry sympathised with the weavers, paying over £1,000 to the lock-outs' fund. Shops gave food; for example, five sacks of flour to make Christmas puddings. A cricket club gave the profits from a match to the fund. People disliked factories for their noise and smoke; they agreed with the weavers that it was healthier to work at home. One clergyman said to loud applause at a weavers' meeting that 'no woman ought to work in a factory. Home was the place for women.' Why did the weavers applaud? A newspaper wrote: 'We have yet to learn that a thing is always better because it is larger. A machine may become injurious as well as useful.' It said that some factory looms were so large that weavers became 'giddy and almost senseless', and that England's large exports were not worth having if they meant '*premature* age' and 'misery' for working people.

On the other hand, another newspaper argued that industry had to be efficient and its costs low, even if work might be unpleasant as a result:

Wherever steam has been found applicable to textile manufactures, our superior energy, enterprise and machinery, as in the cotton trades, have always commanded the markets of the world; and what has been the case in cotton will be the case in silk, unless the energy and enterprise of our manufacturers should be checked, and superior machinery made comparatively useless by the jealousy of competitors, or by the short-sighted policy of the hands themselves.

The newspaper meant that the factories could export ribbons all over the world if weavers did not get wages that were too high. It was saying that steam factories were more efficient than outdoor looms and that factories ought not to be harmed. Why did the paper call weavers 'short-sighted'?

This is really the argument we are having now over the need for higher *productivity*: whether, for example, car workers ought to work faster, so that British cars will be cheaper and sold abroad more easily. It's also the argument about whether we should build huge trawlers rather than small boats that catch less fish but which fishermen find more comfortable. It's the argument between 'efficiency' and those who say 'Small is beautiful'.

For eight weeks the factories of the Bunch of Six were closed, while the weavers demanded payment by the list and the Six refused. James Hart, the leader of the Six, was attacked with what a newspaper called 'violent language and coarse *epithets*' as he walked down Far Gosford Street. The lock-outs received between 7*s* (35p) and 14*s* (70p) a week each from the weavers' fund. This was less than the usual earnings. Life was hard for the Bunch of Six as well. Unable to make ribbons, they risked having to sell their factories. Eventually the threat of bankruptcy forced them to give in to the weavers.

But in April 1859 the weavers again quarrelled with James Hart, when he stopped paying by the list of prices in his factory; and his weavers went on strike. Hart filled his factory with *blacklegs*, paying them 28*s* (£1.40) a week. One weaver said that 'their families were deprived of support by a *skulking* set of underlings, the muffs and duffers of the trade, who were making a harvest just now, when it suited Mr Hart's purpose to pay any sort of money to get people to work'. Weavers were bitterly angry. The chief blackleg, John Mills, (called 'Satin Jack' because he wove satin ribbons), was beaten up. Policemen escorted blacklegs to and from work, but, even so, many were attacked. Seven weavers were imprisoned for one month for this violence.

The magistrates pasted notices on walls in the city warning 55 against violence, but the notices were torn down. On the evening of Monday 6 June over 2,000 weavers waited outside Hart's factory. When the blacklegs came out they and the policemen guarding them were attacked with stones, bricks and watering cans. One policeman was wounded in the back; another's helmet was cut through. Some blacklegs were put

James Hart, the ribbon manufacturers' leader, photographed in 1859

in the lock-up for their own safety and afterwards slept in the factory. More rioters were sent to prison. The magistrates forbade public meetings. Fifty extra policemen were brought in from nearby places to keep order. Within days the city was quiet. Soon, weavers released from prison were welcomed as heroes at weavers' meetings; they wore placards saying: 'These are Paddy Hart's victims.'

In July 1859 Hart gave in, promising to pay his factory weavers by the list of prices. The weavers seemed to have won a great victory, guaranteeing the future of outdoor weaving by raising the costs of factory looms. But within a few months the weavers faced a far tougher battle with Parliament over 'free trade'. They lost that battle, free trade ruined the ribbon industry and the list of prices was swept away.

8 Free Trade, the Great Strike and Emigration

Between 1840 and 1860 Britain was becoming more and more a 'free trade' country. Tariffs were removed from foreign goods and the Corn Laws were ended in 1846. By 1860 silk was the only large British industry still protected from foreign competition. Weavers said that the tariff was fair because Britain did not produce the raw material and therefore was at a disadvantage compared to France because French weavers did not have to buy silk from abroad. But Britain did not grow cotton either, yet the cotton industry was not protected; it was also very efficient and prosperous. One newspaper's reply to the Coventry weavers' argument was that Britain didn't produce any raw materials except coal, iron, fog and acorns.

As the Coventry weavers were fighting the Bunch of Six, in London the *Chancellor of the Exchequer*, W. E. Gladstone, was planning more free trade. He thought it was wrong to protect British industries with tariffs; they raised prices and by lowering competition made it easy to be slack and inefficient. He thought that Britain's history since 1840 proved that free trade reduced prices and made everybody richer.

So in February 1860 Gladstone proposed that all tariffs on foreign manufactures should be ended. This would affect many British people – for example, the makers of gloves – but silk was much the biggest industry involved. Coventry had more to lose than any other town, because more than one-quarter of its people made ribbons and many more relied on the earnings of these people. Men from Coventry visited Gladstone to urge him to continue the tariff on ribbons, even

57

if just for a few years so that weavers might get used to free trade. They said that ribbons were a luxury and so it didn't matter if their price was raised a little.

They did not persuade Gladstone that Coventry ought to have special treatment. Members of Parliament were not convinced either. The MP for Birmingham said that protection 'seemed to enfeeble the mind and reasoning powers' of Coventry weavers. Only fifty-one MPs voted for a proposal to keep the silk tariff for eighteen months. Parliament voted to end the tariff on 3 March.

THE WEAVERS' STRIKE

After the tariff was ended cheap French and Swiss ribbons flooded in, almost twice the quantity being imported in May 1860 as in May 1859. Coventry ribbon manufacturers stopped giving outwork to weavers and some sold off their ribbon stocks at bargain prices because the future seemed so hopeless. More and more weavers were thrown out of work. By June thousands of people were living on loaves given out twice weekly by a group of well-off inhabitants.

At the end of June some manufacturers who had visited the ribbon industries of the continent returned home. They were dismayed by what they had discovered. French and Swiss looms were more efficient and factories and the outdoor trade better organised; weavers worked longer, for less. The returning manufacturers argued that to beat the foreign industries Coventry had to buy new machines and reduce costs.

All the Coventry manufacturers met together for many hours to decide what to do. Some wanted to stick to the list of prices. Most, including the factory owners, wanted to drop it. They could not agree. On 9 July forty-four out of fifty-seven manufacturers published a notice withdrawing their names from the list of prices:

> Because a compulsory uniform List has been used as an instrument of *intimidation* and persecution...
> Because the value of labour depends upon circumstances and must *fluctuate* according to supply and demand...

Because we are now exposed to the competition of manufacturers abroad who have the command of a free-labour market.

On behalf of the weavers, 'J. L.' protested at the reduction of earnings to meet continental competition: 'I protest against being continentalised.... The List has been a lever which has moved the commercial world.'

The manufacturers were saying that earnings had to be lowered to make the ribbon industry more able to compete with foreign looms. They also thought that outdoor weaving might have to end and be replaced by factories that made ribbons more cheaply. In contrast, the weavers were thinking of their standard of living; they knew that if wages were lower they would have to stop eating meat. Besides this, they hated the idea of working in factories, with their discipline and strict hours of work. Which side was right? Were both sides right?

Weavers knew that without a list of prices their earnings would drop greatly. On the other hand the weavers' trade union had no strike fund; all the cash had been spent in the fight with the Bunch of Six. A meeting of weavers was held on Greyfriars Green. One of their leaders, Thomas Maclean, said that the weavers should strike, except those working for the thirteen manufacturers willing to pay by the list of prices. For weavers to stay working for these men would be fair and also the only way the weavers could hope to build up a strike fund – by getting regular payments from those in work. But, as so often in quarrels with employers, the weavers lost their temper, recalling the brutal way the list of prices had just been dropped. The crowd booed Maclean and cheered when some-one called out for a general strike of all weavers.

By the evening of Monday 9 July all looms were stopped, except at two factories. The union committee told weavers to be peaceful, but fights broke out on Tuesday. The factories were surrounded by thousands of weavers; windows were smashed and blacklegs could not enter. One factory owner held weavers off with a sword. The factories had to close. 59

Magistrates were worried about the risk of more violence and whether there would be enough policemen to cope. They banned all meetings except on Greyfriars Green.

The strikers had very little money. Coventry people had supported the weavers before 1860, but they now felt that free trade had altered matters and that to meet foreign competition weavers ought to accept lower earnings. Only £312 were given by Coventry people to help the weavers. Over £1,000 came from trade unions outside Coventry, but, even so, many weavers were starving. By the end of July many strikers were drifting back to work, to 'yells and hisses' from those determined to stay out.

There were many quarrels. For example, John Ludford called Joseph Callow a '*knobstick*'. A newspaper reported: 'The complainant *remonstrated* with him and the defendant became very abusive, put his tongue in the complainant's face and said he would take off his coat and give the complainant what he wanted.' One very complicated case was like many others. Everybody came from the weaving district of Hillfields and most were related to each other. A weaver called Edward Corby, who had gone back to work, met his cousin, Elizabeth Garratt, in the street; she was still on strike and said 'I [Edward Corby] was a bloody thief and my friends a bad lot'. She beat him. Corby's face was bathed with marshmallows by neighbours. Elizabeth Garratt was fined £2, with the option of two months in prison.

Near the end of August the vicar of St Michael's, S. H. Widdrington, appealed to a weavers' meeting to go back to work. 'You have fought the battle of labour against capital at the most fearful odds, in fact when there is no demand for labour.' Loud cries of 'No' greeted his plea that the strike should end. One weaver said that although 'his wife and family had gone without food for three days... he would die for the list if the trade acted with him'. Many weavers agreed with

Opposite: *Weavers lining up for soup in St Mary's Hall, Coventry, in 1861. The women in the foreground are cutting up vegetables and making soup*

him. They wanted the fight to continue. But the facts of starvation had to be faced. Early in September, the strike was over.

MISERY AND EMIGRATION

Most weavers found there was no work for them. Joseph Gutteridge was unemployed for more than a year, like many thousands. He and his wife spent their savings and borrowed money from his brother to get 'a morsel of bread'. In the 1920s one man recalled the 'absolute despair' in the early 1860s when he was twelve or fourteen. 'Hungry men sauntered aimlessly about the streets. . . . The pinched faces of the women told their own tale, while the pathetic march of ragged children with their cans to the soup kitchens spoke volumes.' S. H. Widdrington told of one weaver who:

> Never made any complaint – never let his case be known, but sold article after article to sustain himself, for his pride – perhaps in this instance very blameable – would not let him become a beggar, and at length he died of starvation. . . . He knew of one case where a father and a mother denied themselves a dinner altogether for the sake of giving food to their children, and yet two of the children died of what was called consumption, but was really starvation.

Weavers sold up their bedding, furniture and clothes, and in the end even their looms – which meant (as one person put it) '*severing* the last strand of the cable. . . the sole hope the man has of *retrieving* his former respectable position'. (Gutteridge, luckier than many, managed to keep his loom.) Work was organised for some weavers levelling the city's *common lands*, for 1*s* (5p) a day. Many thousands were kept alive by doles from the Poor Law fund, or by soup provided from nearly £42,000 collected throughout Britain in response to the Coventry relief appeal.

Opposite: *Unemployed weavers levelling Whitley Common and clearing gorse, 1861. Notice the railway bridge and the grindstone, for sharpening hatchets*

EMIGRATION.

NEWS FROM NEW ZEALAND,

BY

JOSEPH WILKINS,

(An Emigrant from Coventry.)

PUBLISHED AT THE REQUEST OF A NUMBER OF FRIENDS.

The following details are published with the view of disseminating authentic information on a subject of vital importance to many of the Working Classes, inasmuch as it affects their prospects in life; and as it is a faithful record of the failures or successes of some, who during the sad distress which has fallen upon the weaving districts, have sought in distant Colonies that honourable subsistence they were unable to obtain in the land of their birth, it must be a deeply interesting subject to all.

Many people are hesitating in this important matter, on account of the imaginary difficulties created by the conflicting nature of the evidence brought before public notice by those, who

> " In all distresses of their friends,
> First consult their private ends."

To any, however, disposed fairly to examine the advantages New Zealand offers to intending Emigrants, this little work, the fruit of close study and careful observation, will undoubtedly prove acceptible.

The earlier transactions in connection with the "settlement," have appeared in a local Newspaper.

COVENTRY:
A. CONNOP, PRINTER, 66, SMITHFORD-STREET.
1863.

Price 1d.

Despairing of finding a better life in Britain, many thousands thought of *emigrating*. When a talk on how to emigrate and what to expect on arrival was given in St Mary's Hall by S. H. Widdrington, the hall was filled long before he began. When he arrived 'men were standing and sitting on each other's backs and shoulders, until masses of human beings were piled up 8 or 10 feet [2½ or 3 metres] high from the floor'. Emigration was carefully planned. Fares were paid by the relief fund. Special services were held in the city churches for the emigrants and special trains hired to take them to Liverpool and Greenwich. At the quayside, relatives and friends waved goodbye to ships filled with people from Coventry.

Many went to the United States, some to weave silk in Paterson, New Jersey; one weaver found his way into the *Confederate* army in Alabama. Many went to farm in Canada, Australia and New Zealand, groups of friends travelling and settling together. One party went to New Zealand. They took parcels of ribbon out with them but found people had too much already. One man complained of high prices and 'hills of greasy clay, much longer and steeper than Hill Top', but added that New Zealand had a better future than Hillfields. Some emigrants wrote home to complain of homesickness, heat, drought and a strange new way of life. Others were happy immediately, one man writing from Brisbane that he had 'never been in better health and circumstances'. He had seen only 'three or four snakes and about half a dozen blacks, but they are all as tame as doves. . . . As for the country, it is like Stoneleigh Park'. Four thousand people left Coventry in 1861 and 1862, one-tenth of the population. The same proportion from Britain's population today would mean five million people, or five times the number of people in Birmingham.

9 The End of Outwork

RIBBONS

The worst part of the slump was over by 1863, but the ribbon trade was never again as prosperous as it had been. French ribbons kept being imported. Women stopped decorating their clothes with ribbon and on their hats used feathers instead. Silkworms died in millions from disease and the price of silk rose. Weavers as skilful as Gutteridge could usually find work, but even he was often unemployed. From September 1890 to March 1891 he earned nothing from weaving. He wrote: 'To keep from starving I was compelled to do odd jobs in violin repairing and inlaid or cabinet work and to sell such articles from the home as could be spared or replaced.'

Gutteridge was now seventy-five, facing the need to work for the rest of his life or enter the hated workhouse. Fortunately, some rich men who knew of his scientific collections and violins arranged to pay him a pension. This made it possible for Gutteridge to retire and to live in some comfort till his death in 1899.

For the last forty years of Gutteridge's life the ribbon industry was dying. Early this century one man wrote about Coventry that 'row after row of houses in these streets still retain as *sole memorial* of better days the top room once specially adapted in every household for the "weaving-room", the walls being practically made of glass'. In 1900 there were only 2,200 ribbon weavers, compared to 10,600 fifty years earlier. Nowadays one ribbon firm, J and J Cash, remains; they weave bookmarks and pictures in silk, in the factory at Kingfield which the firm originally built as 'cottage factories' in the 1850s.

A Coventry ribbon loom of 1870, being used to weave bookmarks for the coronation of Edward VII in 1902

Fortunately for Coventry, soon after the strike and slump of the 1860s, a new industry came into the town and provided jobs. This was the making of bicycles, which in Coventry began in about 1868. The industry boomed when a craze for cycling swept over Britain in the 1880s. In the 1890s Coventry bicycle makers started to put on wheels another invention, the petrol engine. So began the industry which today makes Coventry one of the largest producers of cars in Britain.

OTHER OUTWORK INDUSTRIES

Outwork industries ended because people no longer wished to buy the goods they made, or because factory machines started to make them more cheaply. This is what happened to Dorset buttons. About 1850 a machine was invented which made buttons much more cheaply than outworkers could by hand. It killed the Dorset button industry within a few years. Making nets by outwork lasted longer, because it was difficult to invent a machine that could weave a large mesh. This wasn't done until this century. Nets are still made in Dorset, in a factory in Bridport.

Machines to make stockings, boots and shoes, and nails were all invented between 1850 and 1900. These machines were driven by steam (later, by electricity) and were worked in factories rather than houses; they put the outworkers of Leicester, Northampton and the Black Country out of business. The trousers and shirts once made by outwork are also now made in factories, by large cutting and sewing machines.

Straw-plaiting ended in Bedfordshire because after 1870 plait was imported from Italy, China and Japan. Hatmaking in Luton and Dunstable lasted longer and as an outwork industry. Machines to sew hats were invented in the 1870s, but unlike the machines for boots and nails they were small enough to be worked by hand, like our modern sewing machine. Luton outworkers hired them for 2s 6d (12½p) a week, and so competed with factories. Straw hats were made until people stopped wearing them, in the 1920s.

In Britain a few things are still made by outwork; for example, some women earn money by knitting cardigans and sweaters at home. Can you think of other examples?

LOSS AND GAIN

A lot of outwork was very unpleasant and we can only be glad that machines and factories replaced it. The button-makers of Dorset and the London tailors described by Mayhew, worked very long hours at boring and *repetitive* work for very low pay. The factories that took over their work were healthier places than crowded London rooms or Dorset cottages. Machines made clothes and buttons more cheaply than hands did and so in the long run made everybody richer.

But the Coventry ribbon weavers showed that people preferred to work at home provided that they could earn a good living at it. Weaving was usually very monotonous and tiring work. But working at home, weavers could vary the pace of work to suit themselves. Many working people felt like the Birmingham woman who said: 'Coming late in the morning suits me best, because of getting the children's breakfast.' Unfortunately, factories did not allow workers to come late. It was even possible for outworkers to take days off, perhaps to visit the Show Fair, or to do the household jobs described by a Black Country woman: 'Don't work much on Monday, don't play, but do washing and fetch coals.'

The 'cottage factories' built in Coventry in the 1850s show that it was possible to have the advantages of both steam power and working at home. It is surprising that outworkers elsewhere did not copy the idea; probably they could not afford to.

Between 1830 and 1860 Coventry weavers were better-off than other outworkers. This was partly because of the tariff protecting British ribbons from foreign competition. Most British people thought such tariffs were wrong because they kept prices high. Ending the tariff in 1860 made ribbons cheaper but ruined the Coventry industry. Was this the right thing to do?

How Do We Know?

In writing this book I found out things from:

1. WRITINGS BY NINETEENTH-CENTURY PEOPLE

Lights and Shadows in the Life of an Artisan, JOSEPH GUTTERIDGE, 1893, his autobiography.

Coventry Herald, *Coventry Standard* and *Coventry Times*, weekly newspapers.

Morning Chronicle, a London daily newspaper. It contains Mayhew's writings on outworkers, which were reprinted in 1971 in *The Unknown Mayhew*, edited by E. P. THOMPSON and EILEEN YEO.

Reports on the ribbon trade and public health of Coventry.

The diary of William Andrews, published in *Master and Artisan in Victorian England*, edited by VALERIE CHANCELLOR, 1969.

2. WRITINGS BY PEOPLE OF THE PRESENT DAY

Victoria History of the County of Warwick, volume 8, 1969. A detailed history of Coventry. There will probably be a similar book on your area.

Histories of Bedfordshire and Dorset.

Plenty and Want, JOHN BURNETT, 1966. A detailed history of food and diets.

The Silk Industry of the United Kingdom, SIR FRANK WARNER, 1921. A long History, with many illustrations.

Alive and Well by NORMAN LONGMATE.

Things to Do

1. Find out if any people work at home in your area. Ask them to talk about their work; it may be useful to record them on tape. Compare their lives with those of the outworkers in this book.
2. Compare the family budgets in this book with your own family's. Have prices really gone up or down since 1850?
3. Imagine that you are a weaver 'locked out' in 1858 or on strike in 1860 and write your diary.
4. Hold a class discussion on whether free trade was right or not in 1860.
5. At your reference library look at files of local newspapers in the 1850s and 1860s. Read emigrants' letters back home and see if they were happier after moving.
6. Find a picture of your town in the 1850s and describe how it has changed today.
7. Write and act one of these scenes:
   (a) A meeting to start a friendly society or co-operative shop in your town in the 1850s.
   (b) Weavers trying to persuade Gladstone not to end the ribbon tariff.
   (c) Manufacturers deciding whether to end the list of prices in 1860.
   (d) A party of emigrants sailing for Canada in 1861.
8. Find out if there used to be outworkers near where you live. Compare their lives with those of the outworkers in this book. The *Victoria County History* for your area will help you.
9. Imagine that you are a child in a straw-plaiting school and write your diary for one day.
10. Hold a class debate between manufacturers and weavers in either 1858 or 1860.
11. Write a paragraph for and against allowing foreign cars to be imported into Britain today.

12. Find out if your town used to have a holiday like the Great Fair and write an account of it.
13. Find out which people are paid by piecework today. Write a paragraph comparing piecework to fixed wages, giving the benefits and faults of each.

Glossary

affluent, rich
anvil, large hard block used by blacksmiths for hammering metal on
apprentice, young worker learning the job
autobiography, life of someone written by himself
bankrupt, owing much more than you can pay
blacklegs, people taking the place of strikers at work so as to break the strike
breach of contract, breaking a written promise
brutalising, treating people so badly that they become like animals
building society, business that lends money for people to buy houses
chairman, person in charge of a society or meeting
Chancellor of the Exchequer, member of the government who is in charge of its money
cholera, painful and killing disease
cocoons, woven coverings that protect young silkworms
colossal, huge
commensurate, equal
common lands, lands owned by everyone in a village or town
Confederate, Southern States fighting the North in the American Civil War, 1861–5
consumption, killing disease of the lungs
countenance, face
credit, promise to pay later for things bought now
debris, rubbish
to decline, to say one cannot agree
degrading, making a person seem worthless
dehydration, losing all moisture
deputation, people representing others and arguing their case
despicable, very bad
dignity, a person's respect for himself
disastrous, suddenly making things very much worse

73

dividend, profit or surplus that is shared out

to dominate, to command

emigrating, leaving one's homeland to live abroad

epidemics, outbreaks of disease affecting many people

epithets, adjectives

to fluctuate, to move up and down, like a wave

friendly society, people paying regularly into a fund that helps them during illness

goitres, large swellings on the neck

haggard, looking worried, tired and worn out

hob, stand near fire for a kettle or pan, to keep it hot

imported, brought into a country from elsewhere

impregnated, mixed with

intimidation, causing people to do something against their will by frightening or threatening them

journalist, writer in a newspaper or magazine

kaleidoscope, toy in which one sees beautiful and constantly changing colours and shapes

knobstick, blackleg

lewd, sexually immoral

lock out, keeping workers out of a factory by locking the gates, a sort of strike by employers

ludicrous, causing laughter, ridiculous

memorial, reminder of the past

microbes, germs

mill-dams, built to collect water to drive water-mills

monotonous, boring because the same thing is repeated many times

mosaics, pictures made by fitting pieces together like a jigsaw

multitudes, many people

omnibuses, 'buses, usually pulled by horses

ordeal, worrying time

outdoor, working at home, not in the employer's building

pallet, thin mattress, filled with straw

papier mache, paper mashed up with water and allowed to set hard

paupers, very poor people

to pawn, to borrow money in return for goods which will be given back if the loan is repaid with interest

physiology, knowledge of how the body works

piccolo, musical instrument, made of wood and shaped like a tube, and played by blowing into a hole at one side

piecework, being paid according to the number of things produced, rather than the hours worked

plaited, woven into long strips

Poor Law, a law supposed to make ratepayers look after the poor of their parish either by giving them money or by putting them in a workhouse where in return for work they received board and lodging

premature, happening too early

privies, outside lavatories not flushed with water

productivity, speed of making things

Radical, person wanting big changes and not satisfied with small ones

to remonstrate, to protest

repetitive, constantly repeating

retailer, shopkeeper

retrieving, rescuing

serf, slave

severing, cutting

skulking, hiding like a coward

slump, time when many people are unemployed

snuff, powdered tobacco, sniffed into the nose because of its pleasant smell

sole, only

to solicit, to ask for

surplus, unemployed

superstition, mistaken belief caused by ignorance

to swerve, to turn aside suddenly from a straight line

tariff, tax on imports to put their price up and so protect home industries

temperament, character

twine, thin, strong rope

Index